THE TILTING PLANET

THE TILTING PLANET

Poems

by

DAVID MARSHALL

London Voices
and
The International Brigade Memorial Trust
which is dedicated to keeping alive the memory
and spirit of those who, like David, volunteered
to defend democracy in Spain from 1936-1939.

First published in June 2005
by London Voices
and The International Brigade Memorial Trust
37, Reginald Road, Forest Gate, London, E7 9HS

ISBN 0-9549483-1-9

Back cover photograph by Sid Livingstone

Printed by Intype Libra Ltd,
Unit 3 & 4 Elm Grove Industrial Estate, Elm Grove, Wimbledon,
London SW19 4HE

Available from Marlene Sidaway
37 Reginald Road, Forest Gate, London E7 9HS
www.international-brigades.org.uk

ACKNOWLEDGEMENTS

Cover design and photo layout	Tan Khokhar
Typesetting	Barbara Tucker
Editor	Marlene Sidaway
Editing and layout	Gillian Oxford

Marlene Sidaway is David's partner, an actor and writer, and Hon. Secretary of the I.B.M.T.

*Gillian Oxford has published her own and others' work in a series of anthologies from **London Voices**, a leading poetry workshop.   Additionally she has published **Touching Tomorrow**, **The Stone in the Ring** and **What is the Time now**. She has also co-written traditional and historical stories for the dyslexic reader, published by Heinemann Educational.*

Dedicated to Marlene Sidaway

My thanks to Andy Croft, Gillian Oxford
and the members of London Voices
for their encouragement and help

LIST OF ILLUSTRATIONS

CONTENTS

Dave Marshall, 2004

INTRODUCTION

London, May, 2005

I have written poems all my life, and they have reflected my life and the things that were occupying my mind at the time, they tell of my inner self, and my reactions to my personal world and to the greater world and events through which I have lived.

Apart from "Retrospect" which I wrote just after my return from Spain in 1937, I have not sought publication until now – it seems that at the age of 89 I no longer feel possessive or diffident about my work.

Perhaps I was reluctant to share my deepest thoughts with others, and yet I always hoped they would be read by "ordinary" men and women, and would strike a cord with a shared experience of work, striving for a better life, dreaming great dreams and having them shattered by the battering of living in this world of our making.

I hand my thoughts on to a younger generation, make of them what you will, I hope they spark off new thoughts and better dreams, which may, in the long fullness of time be fulfilled.

David Marshall

Spain

Members of the Tom Mann Centuria with their
banner outside the Karl Marx barracks in Barcelona,
September 1936.
*Left to Right: Sid Avner, Nat Cohen, Ramona, Tom
Wintringham, George Tioli, Jack Barry, Dave Marshall*

Retrospect

Go back –
Six feet of snow on the Aragon front;
While here
Kids slide in the roadways
Steadied feet thudding in the gutters:
Ice blurs
The red orange blue of neon lights –
The harlot shops invite.
But there
The café lights blink and blacken
Ribs tighten, skin grows ware –
After the momentary adjustment
A fumbling for the tasteless glass –
A startled touch of warm-whorled fingers
A greedy intake of smoke
The lung-shock battens the nerves –
Strange faces glow intimate
Red-arc'd by the fitful cigarette.

Distant shots
Snap at lit windows –
Tenseness strangles the blood –
The walls reverberate
From an anti-aircraft in the church next door
That coughs dully, cough, cough…

Vienen los aviones, ay ay,
Los aviones, says some woman –
Carven deu, tancat la boca …
Then the bombs

Belching earth-pits
Quagging the ground,
One two three sudden,
Four, wait wait wait five,
SIX god that's it

Shattering, rumbling racket
Glass smashing and one thin endless scream.
Then a dullness in the head,
We stand over the table,
A glass falls, rings,
The air tastes of the Metro.
The cigarettes are all out.
A no-sex voice from the street
Cries Sanidad Sanidad
Christ let's get out of this ...
Ay, alli mucha de la muerte hay,
Y aqui, que hay mejor.

I have stood to upon some lousy dawn

[At Jarama, Moors crept up behind the sentries
guarding the bridge, slit their throats and
mutilated them. The bridge was lost and as a
result, many men were killed.]

I have stood to upon some lousy dawns
When even insects slept
Demanded friend from foe – a silly drill
No army reg. nor proper polished button
Could guard against the dark patrol
The silent knife that slits the gullet
And gushes blood in all our cavities
The fascist pig is rooting in our garden
And many men were cut and cut again,
Their bollocks shoved in broken mouths.
We had not guessed at this atrocity
But Franco chose to use these infidels
To strengthen his most Christian crusade.

I sing of my comrades

I sing of my comrades
That once did sing the Internationale
In that great choir at Albacete
Before the battle. Rank after rank
Of the young battalions
They came from every corner of the earth
So many men from distant lands
Who took to arms in the defence
Of Spain's Republic.

Madrid the magnet that drew us all
Along slow roads to Spain – at last a star
For desperate men, sensing the gathering storm
And we that fought to warn a watching world
Were called false prophets
Yet fought for the poor of the world.

Our lullabies were soldiers' songs
Sung by sad women to the sons of the fallen.
And remembered in Remembrance Day long past
After the thudding drum and shriek of bugles
I listened to the slow lament
For brothers, sons and lovers lost.
It is the sadness in the singing,
The undertones of woe,
The deep vein of grief
That throbs throughout my generation.

Dave Marshall in Spain, 1936

I wish I were back...

I wish I were back in the trenches round Madrid
Along with the chicos, among the strangeness of
tongues:
Strong in my body, testing it thus and thus,
Half wondering that my flesh can bear these
things.

Glad in my loneliness, wrapt in my alien
thoughts;
My quaintness cloaking me, like cold air
Stirring on the skin when putting off familiar
clothes –
Just as I stepped out of my time-pocked life
Into this.

Then the terror stript me of bewilderment,
Left me shrinking and shell-less, my soul
A slim white worm, curling blindly in fear:
Only one direction to my consciousness,
To kill before I was killed, and glad to die
That our new world begins.

And the tanks lurching like monsters
Stiff-shouldered through the slime,
The horrid black concussion of bombs
Spouting earth skywards,
And the vicious shrapnel
And the hideous chatter of machine-guns
All these could not shatter our resolution.

War

La Toussaint, 1. 11. 45.
St. Lazaire, pendant l'oraison funèbre, pour les
morts tombés pour notre victoire.

At St. Lazaire for the funeral oration for those
fallen during the liberation, 1945.

Gift from a grateful Government

The M.O.D. regrets to report
He died as he ought
Fighting for democracy.

We return his remains -
In this bottle his brains
That ached with dreams and schemes

Some teeth, still sound,
That bit your breast and mound
So your sweet head turned
Your mouth made sounds
And all your body burned.

His lips, so fond of kissing
Are missing:
Here is a finger
That once did, loving, linger
Upon your throat and shoulder.

There was, of course, none bolder.
He was a model soldier
As these spare parts attest
We couldn't find the rest.

So cherish the children of his seed
Who one day may repeat his deed -
Avenging his evisceration
In the service of a caring nation.

I have lived in a time of heroes

I have lived in a time of heroes
And heroines; of great objectors
To subjection and persecution.

I have rubbed rough shoulders
With unnumbered unknown soldiers
Dead in their tens of thousands.

The working men who saved Madrid,
Those lads that fell at Alamein
At Arnhem and at Stalingrad.

These were my comrades, my companions,
Civilians, conscripts, partisans,
Who did great deeds to win hard victory.

In unremembered graves they lie
Untrumpeted, their songs forgotten
Our children are not taught their history.

And you forget them at your peril
For though you fight as well as they
You'll be betrayed, as we were.

Where e're you walk in foreign fields

Where e're you walk in foreign fields
You're treading upon dead men
And if you go by car or coach
Upon the open road
Think of when the stukas came
Bombing refugees and soldiers
And in the ditches dead men.

Or you may seek the cleaner beach
Wherein your kids may safely bathe
And as you splodge in Norman waters
Remember the craft which carried
The already dead –
Those yet alive
Tripping and slipping on the pebbles
Staining the sand one red
You would have thought that so much blood
Would thicken this thin water
All along the strand lay dead men

Or when you take the Dunkirk ferry
Remember the human snake
That fought for footing on the turning tide
This khaki arm flung out for saving
By the small boats that ran aground
Loaded in this bloodied water
And in the dunes the dead men.

Those dead were once your dads and granddads
Or some one else's sons and lovers
Such likely lads
O the dead men
Never forget the dead men.

Reflections

Barge Match

Silent witness

Does the fallen feather tell
How far she flew, in winter lands or summer,
Or if she lagged, or led the flock.

Does it tell of long migrations
Of glad arrival and soft nesting,
Or panic flutter in distress.

Of none of these can it speak.
It lies there to be fingered
By another indescribable mortal.

And the patient explorers of wrecks –
What can they tell from their scraping
And their scrupulous listing of relics.

What of the bills and manifests
That listed her many ventures;
The names of her crews and destinations.

How did she swim in heavy weather,
Riding-out the shouldering seas –
Or did she put her men in peril.

Gone is the wonder of her wandering
The maps that caught her men with magic
The nightly yarns of her survivals.

All her service lies in silence:
Only the stitching nails persist,
And the lines of her swimming timbers in the
mud.

And the despoilers of empty buildings
Riffling the litter
What can their scavenging uncover.
For dust and web mask all endeavour
Blur the echoes and apparitions
Of the planners and the lovers in this place.

Mute the sharp hammers, the men disbanded,
No colours, calls, nor revels are apparent –
All scattered is their enterprise.

And though the dissectors of corpses
Quickly discover the causes of death
They never uncover the causes we lived for.

Reflections

Watching black water
Blurring scrambling the images
Scattering the reflections.
Recalling my rovings,
Arrivals and departures,
Damages and jubilations.

Dredging remembrance
In a gilded slither of faces, places,
My crews, my good companions, –
They travel in different ways and distant.

None are now in this great haven
Of those I knew when I was younger,
As I watch black water, weighing
This last ineluctable venture.

I have bent my life my way

I have bent my life my way
Against tongues and biddings:
So have I done some little well.

Now I am indeed old
I know I was not so splendid
As the present young…..
My way was not the whole way.

I had reason to take a hard road
By a high star shining –
Men since have circled brighter,
All heaven within their reach.

Every silver star for taking:
Had I only known
I should have unfixed my staring
And looking in another's eyes
Might have seen smaller, but warmer, worlds.

David Quixote

I have fought fantastic giants
And, constantly in battle –
Killed some with ease, some hardly –
But was never yet defeated.

One day, weary with little winning
And noting the absence of cheering
I turned to look at my brothers
To see if they matched my stubbornness –
There was no one by my side.

All were absorbed in husbandry,
In the warm lands
And then I knew –
Other men didn't need dragons,
And I should have to learn
To hammer this savage sword
Into a simple sickle.

Not Xanadu

Not Xanadu, but Xanten-on-the-Rhine
Was where I last heard Nightingales: they sang
Unseen among the bushes and the trees
Made bare by our bombardment.
Sentries listened, and those that could not sleep,
Dreading the coming dawn, felt even lonelier.

The Larks that sang when I was young
Lift no more from moor or meadow.
They flew up 'till the rim of heaven
And poured their song upon the thirsting earth.

The Nazis could not kill the nightingales
But peace and pesticides put paid
To birdsong and brought about
The silence of the Larks.

Challenge

Challenge

I call on great Dagon
And his six legions of demons
On Mammon devourer of children
And Pluto, evil lord of hell
And all their minions in line descendent;
I call on them all
On Kings and decorated captains
All conquerors and commanders
And rank on rank behind their regiments
Of Politicians, Priests and Pressmen
On all those suave deceivers
Those silky, smiling tigers
Who promised paradise and gave us wilderness
Making their wealth our woe
So their profit is our loss,
And all our lands are rifled by these rascals.

I call you now with greatest voice
Cry halt against the harrying of my people.
With tripling clarion and harshest trumpet
All our unsung heroes will arise
And stand in solid squadrons at our side
And end forever your dominion.

And we shall lift like mountain sides
And toss you from our shoulders
Like leviathan heave
And tumble you all to destruction.

Beaten

Who tore out their tongues, they cannot speak,
These mutilates that hammer in my head
So I stand stunned by all their clangour
And cannot tell the terror of my dreaming.

Why do they mine the caverns of my skull
Down to the bruising bone,
No treasure-trove can they discover –
Only the dust and dross of my despair.

Whatever did I thieve from Heaven
That these vultures thus torment me
Whichever Islam did I slander
Could sanctify such hard revenge.

How is my heart so torn like fabric
Like a flag made mad by wind
So I stagger like a man demented
And feel the earth beneath me shudder.

Will they never cease their plunders
Down their picks and heavy sledges
And leave me to the bite of silence.

Ease will not come, nor peace, nor sleep;
They tunnel in my brain for ever
And make a devastation of my soul.

Scrimshaw *(How to write a poem)*

First find that special pebble on the beach.
Then turn it over
See the seethe of insects of the sea
Delve and dive into the sealing sand
Then dig deep
Past fathom five where fathers lie
Past broken timbers and bronze cannon
Down to the graves of whales
To the secret cemeteries of the deep
Where sleep the elephant seals
Amid whose tumbled bones
Glint tusk-like teeth
On which at last I scratch
These my words.

The vivid crimson of the rose
Darkens at dusk, as the light goes.
The scarlet start of blood on skin
Cakes and blackens, as life goes.

While break of day revives the rose
There is no dawn for dead men.

Remembrance of things past

Middlesbrough –
Teeside Transporter Bridge

Deep in the basement of my brain

Deep in the basement of my brain
I keep my dreams – a library
Of lantern-slides and photographs
Of all the presences and places
From my childhood times. And there by night,
Prowling the corridors of sleep, my thoughts
unravel,
Fingering the shelves; looking for clues
For any reason why
I had to leave my little kingdom,
My infant realm, my sweetest Eden –
Be conscript in this adult world –
Trained to ape their alien ways
And taught to live their language.

I did not understand my elders,
They wished on me a world I did not want
That they too did not want yet had endured
They had too early learned defeat,
And had left it too late for mutiny.

I knew my world with instant eyes
Before I had an alphabet,
Felt it, tasted, had no fear –
Played my part upon that vivid stage
In that sweet season had no need of words

But the present will not match the past.
And now by night I improvise
In the laboratories of sleep
Piecing clips of the silent past
Vainly trying to revive
The natural wonder of that buried time.
But the fragments will not run together,
The patterns are scattered past all repair
There's no translation from the then to now,
But the puzzlement and hurt remain
Through all my nights and days.

Rive as you will at ivy on a wall
The rootlets cling to the brickwork
And so the imprints of that time persist
To underpin the structure of my being.

Indifferent time drifts dust upon the past
Yet still there glints a spark amid the silt
That trips the hidden shutters of my mind
Reveals that still I dream of Eden

Middlesbrough

An old man now, why should I sing
Of the town where I was born and taught,
Yet sing I must, though hoarse my voice is
And harsher made by savage anger
At the degradation of my people
The rack and ruin of all their labour.

Long, long ago I left the North
Under no moon, on a night of midsummer
Turning my back on the Northern Star,
And headed for London
Leaving bitter Tees for sweeter Thames
And prayed that all went well with me.

A-top a bank, by weeping willows
their leaves as long as ladies fingers –
I lingered, thinking to look my last
On the place that gave me no contentment
And half-afraid I'd stayed too long.

A lake of darkness filled Tees Valley
Braided with loops and strings of street-lamps
Like the riding lights of a vast armada
Or as if beneath that black lagoon
Lay half-submerged a live atlantis
Stealing its light from the stars above
A glittering City of Steel.

I heard the sullen stubborn growl
Of furnace, forge and rolling mill
And over that bass in mad cadenzas
The stutter of buffers and couplings
From shunted trucks in yards and sidings.

As if before a night attack
With thudding mutter of muted drums
And staccato spitting of trumpets
Urging the trudging legions on.
And I heard the laboured gasping breath
Of a thousand men on night shift -
Like brazen beasts in the metal sheds
Tended and fed by midnight men.

Forgetting the lean and famine years
And all the bitterness and woe –
With so many men made idle
In my home-town alone; laid off
To sign the book and draw the dole,
Twice a week in shuffling queue
And twice a day for dockers
To say "No work",   show forty card –
That yellow badge of the unwanted –
To pocket a pittance, the market price
Of forgotten jobless hopeless men.

And these were chaps who'd earned big money
Handling metal – furnace-men; first-hand
smelters
Charge-hands, rollers, sample-passers
The names and terms - like billet and pig

And soaking pit come tumbling out
And all the Half-remembered trades
Of Fitters, Smelters, Metal Dressers
Riveters, Platers, Windy Drillers
A grand roll-call of skills discarded
All tossed to scrap their occupations
Dead letters on a Cenotaph.

And I forgot the barefoot kids
Picketing the Transporter as the shifts came off,
Raggy-arsed they begged for bait
For a bit of bread from a Tommy Tin.

For evil days were come again
In the silent valley of the Tees
And I shall die 'ere they revive.

Introspection

Outsider

I dwell in the outskirts:
But from maps and observation
Well know men's intricate cities.

I understand their tongues and music:
In masks, in disguises
Have forayed often in their territory.

I have grown quite like them -
Taken part in their ceremonies
And been approved, but not discovered.

I even loved one of their women - once, -
But she perceived my strangeness
And turned away to safety.

Loneliness sits aslant the mirror

Loneliness sits aslant the mirror
Not to be in the picture
Not to be present where reality is
To eye the world askance
To not partake of pain or pleasure
To keep in shadow when there is sun
Not to sing when there is music
Fear to touch when there is giving
Not to give when there is touching
It's anorexia of the soul.

We mask our dreams

We mask our dreams lest people laugh –
Like lonely men stroke photographs
Wishing the flesh to warm and quicken
Start and stir beneath our fingers,
But the picture will not leave the page
Nor ever lose its cold dimension
When silence sits around us
We are left with only longing.

Where will you sleep tonight?

Where will you sleep tonight in this hard season
O girl that wears three rings in either ear
And silver studs in tender lip
Where will you sleep tonight?
In some shop doorway marked by passing dogs
Part sheltered from the prying wind.

At Covent Garden sitting at ease in glittering
tiers,
How easily the wealthy weep
For a factory girl called Carmen,
Or Mimi with that dreadful cough
And Butterfly, a single mum
Let down by careless lover
How easily the tears can flow
For Violetta, alone and lost in bed-sit land.

The taxis come the taxis go
The polished Bentleys whisper past
Taking their women to warm beds.
Where will you sleep tonight
In this hard season.

The barge

Barge for sale

She awaits a strange captain
To alter her intention
For a last magical journey.

She will sail for the happy isles
Where troubled hearts find freedom
And no leaves fall like tears.

After bright springs
And lonely voyaging
She will come to still harbour.

After remembered summers
And tempests of autumn
She will come at last to haven.

Storms will cease, and rains ease
And proud as any swan
She will swim on soft water.

Thames Sailing Barge
"Jock"

I am beginning a journey

I am beginning a journey –
My last. I shall never arrive –
I will be travelling 'til death.

It will be a strange, exciting journey
With friends I have not met before:
And myself, each day a stranger.

It is an inevitable voyage,
And whatever wind, or tide, or water,
Nothing can deflect its purpose.

Most men go this road unready:
Provisioned and prepared
I travel alone, and further.

I shall never arrive: I shall be
Later than many, sooner than some;
But I will be journeying.

In this my palace on the water

In this my palace on the water
In this my timber kingdom
I sit in empty silence.

No troupers, troubadours nor tumblers
No masques, dancers nor musicians
None revel in my galleries
In my pavilions is no laughter.

Only by night, at the rain's insistence
Arrive my shadowy courtiers
Sliding and turning to older melodies –
Past partners, first loves
My scattered comrades
My lost, my glorious brothers.

For how long yet must I vigil keep
Intent to the ring of a distant horn,
Or the lapping ripple of a boatman, sculling
To wake a king who sleeps in Avalon.

My Palace on the Water

Love poems

Desiderium

I shall never know the black dancer,
Her limbs four silky fishes.
My fingers will not follow
Lip, lobe and eyelid,
Nor ski the swift slopes
Of throat and rib and shoulder.

She will not stir as the reading whorls
Whisper in loin and navel.
I shall not see her eyes stilled,
Her turning mouth.
I shall not hear her love sounds
Nor taste her sweet salts.

There will be no homecomings:
She will not be at my house.

But I shall always have the thought
I should have asked her.

Truth is a fluttery cobweb

Truth is a fluttery cobweb,
I cannot make it quiver
I wished with a web of words
To mesh my jewelled fly
Fondle, feel and probe her parts
Know she was truly mine.

But the earth beneath me trembled
The world outside distracted me:
And when I looked to take my will of her
She had loosened my loving bonds
And suddenly was able to fly away.

I courted a Princess of Egypt

I courted a princess of Egypt,
Coiling her tresses over her breasts,
Kissing her black and crimson parts.

Could I but utter like trumpets
I could not tell her beauty
As velvet as dolphin dancing.

In that strange Territory
I trod like a tiger
None could outdo me.

Recalled to the Republic
I found I was forgotten
My properties impounded
My name erased from monuments.

I was left with little treasure
A necklace of Nubian Ivory
Which I send to rest, on your warm breast,
And remind you of Mark Anthony.

The lover

I sit, at night, writing a poem
To say though I left you, I love you still –
Yet where is the truth of my pain.

Did I dread the friends,
The tongues that turned against us –
No man's word disturbs me now.

Was it for son or daughter
Who must live their own lives –
They do not need me now.

Was it for love of my wife –
For haven, or a hiding place –
I sit in her house like a ghost.

Was it for my work – I do not know –
It is all, all that remains.
I have sold my heart to a demon
And shall fight him in torment for ever
And that is the truth of my pain,
As I sit, writing a poem to you.

Love Reincarnate.

How many lives ago did I know you,
You who seem to be the essence of myself?
Did we mate in some Jurassic jungle,
Clumsy in our contorted couplings?
Did we love in the shadows of a cold cave,
With beasts howling outside?
Did we grapple with our passions under Syrian
stars
Whilst Egyptian invaders prepared to spear us?
Or were you some Turkish potentate,
And I your favourite concubine?
Coming nearer to our own times,
Did you sport in medieval inn, with me,
Your serving wench, who served your board and
bed?
And why, in this present incarnation,
Have we been born out of step,
So that you had loved and married
Ere I was born,
And our brief bliss, the timeless moment of our
loving,
Became the source of pain and bitter strife,
And had to end?
Will we meet again?
Will we fuse and burn together in the universe,
With cosmic brilliance?
Or are our paths, like comets seldom seen, about
to part?
Last week I heard of your death,
And a part of me died too.

48

Early works

Speed fiend

Feel the judder of struts a-snarl
Writhe from the lilling tongue of tyre
Rubber-lipped gobbling the miles:
Feel the bars
Shudder at wrist and shoulder,
Throb to the road with speed:
Feel sinews torn
To hot wire; the drag of heart
Battering at bruised ribs:
Feel blood pump hot, feel guts molten
Twining to knots of fire;
Sense the scream
The agony of nerve and muscle –
Feel thy body seared with speed,
Feel thy back sprung steely,
Strong to tear and wrest and pound out speed;
Maddened in strength,
Feel the jar and jerk to speed
The spit of rubber, pouncing
Tearing at miles,
Fleeing arrow-swift the storm of feet
The piston-stamp:
While I
Swift on thin wheels
Storm at the gates of my Desire.

Daphne

In the thick branches
All pendant globulous pearl
Daphne,
Slim-stumbling, sun-haired
Even in words a loveliness

With a rasp of leaves
Panting
Tawny Apollo.

A spent huddle of limbs,
Terror at eyes,
Tight-throated –
Then his keen fingers on her brown flesh,
Teeth bruising that soft mouth
Now slack-lipped and quivering:
Satin breasts crumpled on his ribs –
Once
Torn by his roughness
A sob of utter surrender.

Afterwards a stillness
Even no tremor of eyelids
Bodies drenched in dark cool wells,
Grass stirs, the music ebbs,
-----Night falls like a curtain.

Last Waltz – Modern

Brek, ek ek, coax coax
Croaks the hoarse sax –
Cigarettes nipped,
Sleak heads by the door
Cluster, turn,
Ordered by the throaty saxophone,
Irregularly presenting
The regular formulae,
Eyes, mouth, nose, set complete
On the official blank
As if ready for filing…

After the walk home –
Stumbling over the tussocks behind the
allotments,
Not speaking, dry-throated,
Fearful for interruption – then jerkily –
"Sit down a minute".

Lying in the harsh grass
Not soon comfortable on the lumpy turf
Cold, tired, strange in clothing
Holding each other in awkward arms…

The star web shimmers with unseen spider feet
Night's blue gong
Insidiously reverberates
Echoing back
The incessant shunting in sidings
The ravening batteries of coke-ovens mouthing to
heaven

But here
Here it is wind-rapt
Fenced in by the stubborn hedge and jagged huts
They feel only the stillness underground
Hear only the grass noises…
Aloneness has them close,
They are warmer.

His hand creeps down
Slow, tense, his fingers pluck her dress
Her skin roughens to his coldness…

Yea, those hot moments –
Fumbling to the crotch of her legs,
Throat-breathing
His elbow levering her bended knees apart
"O Jack, I'm so scared, Jack, you'll be
careful…"
"Yes, yes, you know it's o.k. –
Be quiet, keep still, kiss me."

Yea, all this
Completely lapsed and filed away
Forgotten in dusty cabinets of sleep
Till 8 a.m. sharp
On with the motley mask
The same blank form awaiting its completion
And the checking red initial
Of lipstick.

Mount Grace

On the edge of the moors, near my home, there is
a ruined priory, called Mount Grace. Hidden in
nettle and bramble is a well, into which one has
to drop a leaf, and wish.

I plucked my love an ivy leaf
(She will not come, she will not come)
Pinned-on my heart with a hooky pin
And dropt them in the wishing-well
(I wish she will, I wish she will)

My heavy heart sank like a stone
(She will not come, she will not come)
It pulled the glossy ivy down
And hid beneath it from the chill
(I wish she will, I wish she will)

The silver pin it bites my heart
And makes a crimson tear to start
(She will not come, she will not come)
O take the wings of a magic bird
Fly fast and far o'er sea and hill
(I wish she will, I wish she will)

Put thy hand into the water
(She will not come, she will not come)
Pick my heart from out the water
Pluck the pin and loose the leaf
Kiss the scar and make it well
(I wish she will, I wish she will).

Night Thoughts

Wind-walking I begot it…
This is my dream…

So I built me a boat
Stubborn-ribbed:
Thumbed from my dreams
The plans: thus and thus
With these lean hands,
Subtly curved and moulded
Craftily constructed her –
Strake-flanked, keen-prowed –
Ready
To take the sea.

Cliff-breasted,
Lamp-nippled is my mistress –
Her skin blue-tinted,
Veined whitely, restlessly –
Yet based in stillness.
But I took me another
A mate of my own kind –
Alike in many ways…
In this resonant womb,
Ripple-pulsed,
Planted a seed
Deep in the sea's flat belly –
A womb within a womb.

And after, Quien sabe? ...
Wind-walking I forgot it.

So I go home
Through yellow-drenched fingers
Spread on black satin,
Lamp-jewelled.

Tacky tires in the wet
Spit past, shrink in distance;
Stillness quivers, and the wind runs
At my throat.

Ach I am home
There is no change
Look in the mirror
I am still the same.

Y.C.L.

After the ceaseless savagery of the rain
Stabbing the jet roads, lamp-ribbed,
After the car-bugs spitting sleekly past
Have splashed our damp legs, their yellow antennae
Searching, lancing the darkness…
After the committees, the many decisions –
We go quietly home…

All these nights are one to us, there is no rest –
Sometimes there's satisfaction…
The victories are for the townsfolk…
But afterwards
There is a redirection and a tougher determination
Urging us on, restless…

O, we are stubborn fighters, Spain has taught us that;
We were too young for the other lessons –
Yet each night we learn;
Each one his private failure taking home,
Painfully dissecting, probing the flaws:-
This loneliness is bitter, but out of it, comes the steel.

But leaning on the doorpost, tired,
In the darkness, under the rain,
The failures are forgotten; the friendly faces

Surge in our hearts. We think of Dave in jail
Jim at the front – of all the thousand thousands
Manning our distant brigades…
Of those who also fight
Fiercer yet more secret wars
Here in our town – struggles in their hearts
In their homes;
Of all the weary bodies laid for resting,
Rumps and ribs compact on crumpled sheets –
Shirt or pyjama-wrapt
Still fettered in the one escape…
We sense these shadowy legions
Their multitudinous gutturals flung back from
windy corners
Their strong fingers fumbling at the knot
That holds us all to earth –
In the drenched darkness we hear them:-
"We have hammers for our fetters
For our knots we have the sickle."

For ourselves we have the night.

Afterthought

The tilting planet

The tilted planet springs us into springtime,
The star of Venus lifts, her sparrows chatter
And in my garden all the plantings creep
From fugitive shoot to leaf, from bud to flower
Till all the jubilant earth erupts
And spits itself to seeding.

But I am past that season, into winter,
Where seeds and dreams all hide in silence
And hardened by that frosty sleep, await
The constant revolution of the world.

For move it does, this patient waiting earth
Till restless men will it to tilt
And spin us all to brighter, better springs.